Hymns

by
Brenda Gallant

Set to music by Harry Hicks

Published by:
Clifftop Music
"Clifftop,"
30, Seaview Road,
Mundesley,
Norfolk.
NR11 8DH.

Tel.: 01263 722757
email: harry.hicks147@btinternet.com

Hymns by Brenda Gallant
Music by Harry Hicks

A special day	1
All our lives	2
As you travel	3
Christ is coming	4
Christ is risen	5
Christ is the only answer	6
Come with gladness	7
Creation	8
Redemption	9
Emmanuel, the true expression	10
Finished	11
For those disciples	12
Go forth	13
God loved the world	14
God shows His love	15
God's promise	16
God's Spirit	17
In the beginning	18
Is it well?	19
Let me tell you tonight/wonderful place	20
Long long ago	21
Long, long ago	22
Love – joy – peace	23
Mary and Joseph	24
No other way	25
Oh flee	26
Oh who is this	27
Our Saviour	28
Praise the God of truth and love	29
Seek	30
Slumbering in a manger	31
The light	32
The Lord is here	33
The manger	34
The Saviour Christ	35
This happy Christmas Day	36
Upon the cross	37
Watching, waiting	38
We thank thee	39
What a wonderful salvation	40
When the Lord	41
Where is he?	42
Where oh where	43
Why seek the living	44
Your God is here	45
Your life is borrowed	46

1 A special day

Brenda Gallant
Harry Hicks

A special day, a special day, When God came down with men to stay. He came to save us all from sin, The human heart to enter in. Special day! Special day! When God came down with men to stay.

2. He came a Babe in manger laid,
The One whose hands the world had made,
He bore our sicknesses and woe,
And tasted every earthly throe.
Special day! Special day!
When God came down with men to stay.

3. A special day! A special day!
When Jesus bore our sins away!
They nailed Him to a cruel tree,
He suffered there for you and me.
Special day! Special day!
When Jesus bore our sins away.

4. He rose again, and left the grave,
This sinless Saviour came to save,
He died for you to set you free,
That you with Him might ever be.
Special day! Special day!
When Jesus bore our sins away.

5. A special day, a special day,
When Christ returns with great array,
the trump shall sound, the dead arise
To meet the Saviour in the skies.
Special day! Special day!
When Christ returns with great array.

Music © 2013 Harry Hicks
Words © 1993 Brenda Gallant

2 All our lives

Brenda Gallant
Harry Hicks

*All our lives are like a journey
On a vast and changing sea,
There are many dangers lurking,
Hazardous to you and me.
Waves that seek to overwhelm us,
Currents strong to suck us down;
How we need a chart and compass,
That we may not sink and drown.*

2. God the powerful Creator,
Made us for His own delight,
He, Himself, has made provision
So that we may sail aright.
   Christ the Lord has gone before us,
   Faced the storms of life alone;
   If we take Him as our Saviour,
   He will lead us safely on.

3. He has give us chart and compass,
Light to guide us on our way,
If we read His word, the Bible
We will never want to stray.
   There is comfort in our sorrow,
   Guidance for our wandering feet,
   Shelter when we face temptation
   When the storms of life we meet.

4. Open then His word and read it,
Pray that through it He will speak,
If you need this free salvation,
You will find it when you seek.
   Then, together you will journey
   On towards the harbour light,
   Which itself is but the entrance
   To the heavenly mansions bright.

Music © 2013 Harry Hicks
Words © 2013 Brenda Gallant

3 As you travel

Brenda Gallant Harry Hicks

[Piano sheet music]

As you tra-vel o'er life's sea, Who will your com-pan-ion be?
As you push to-ward the shore, Who's the hand up-on the oar?
Do not jour-ney on your own, Batt'-ling through the waves a-lone,
Take the Sav-iour as your guide, 'Til you reach the o-ther side.

2. When the storms of life abound,
Let your faith in Christ be found,
He will then your anchor be,
Save you from the angry sea.
   You may trust Him with your all,
   He will never let you fall,
   You are safe with Him aboard,
   Loving Saviour, friend and Lord.

3. Be your voyage long or short,
Take great comfort from this thought;
He has promised to be near,
Giving comfort, joy and cheer.
   So invite Him to your bark
   Do not journey in the dark,
   He will chart the troubled sea,
   And your pilot ever be.

4. Praise Him for His wondrous love,
And those mansions up above,
He has promised to prepare,
He will guide you safely there.
   Trust Him now, invite Him in,
   He will deal with all your sin,
   Come and live within your heart,
   And His own sweet peace impart.

Music © 2013 Harry Hicks
Words © 2013 Brenda Gallant

4 Christ is coming

Brenda Gallant
Harry Hicks

Lyrics under music:
Christ is coming, Hallelujah! Christ is coming back again,
He is coming as He promised, He will take His power and reign.
Are you ready for His Advent, Will He find you watching here,
Are you washed and cleansed and waiting, In His glory thus to share.

2. Christ is coming, Hallelujah,
Christ is coming back again,
Every eye will then behold Him,
Every voice take up the strain,
Those who set at nought and scorned Him,
Those who cursed His precious Name,
They will bow the knee before Him,
Overwhelmed in guilt and shame.

3. Christ is coming, Hallelujah,
Christ is coming back again.
Will you welcome His appearing,
Will you join the glad refrain?
Even so, oh come, Lord Jesus,
Come and claim your chosen bride,
Come and take us up to glory,
There forever to abide.

Music © 2013 Harry Hicks
Words © 2013 Brenda Gallant

5 Christ is risen

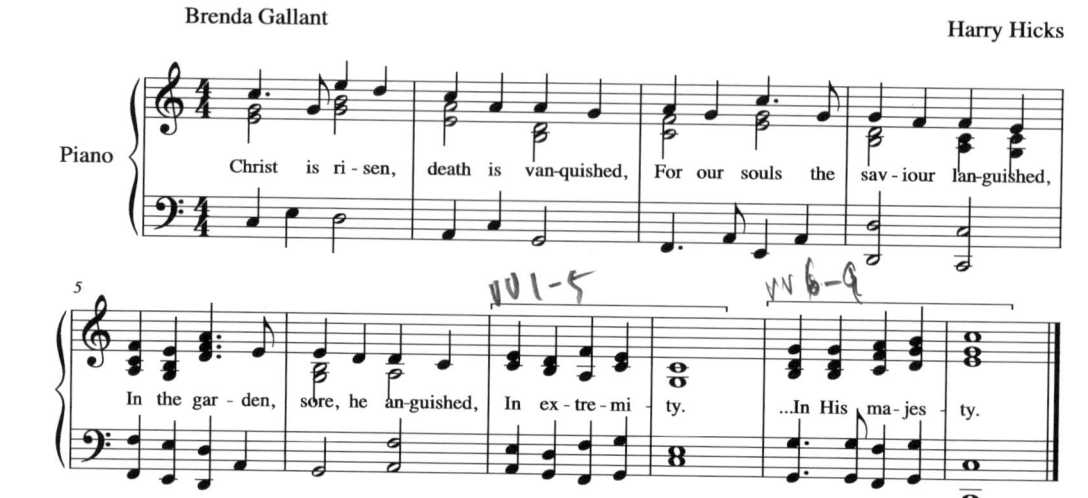

Brenda Gallant

Harry Hicks

Christ is ri-sen, death is van-quished, For our souls the sav-iour lan-guished, In the gar-den, sore, he an-guished, In ex-tre-mi-ty. ...In His ma-jes-ty.

2. Christ is risen, how He suffered
As his sinless self He proffered,
All He had to God He offered,
   In humility.

3. Christ is risen, sin's grip broken,
It is finished, He has spoken,
Shed His blood, that blessed token
   Of eternity.

4. Christ is risen, tomb is bare now,
For His body is not there now,
This good news is here to share now,
   With integrity.

5. Christ is risen, task completed,
Satan's tactics all defeated,
Now in heaven Christ is seated
   In His majesty.

6. Christ is risen, Jubilation!
He has purchased our salvation,
Let us praise Him with elation
   And in ecstasy.

7. Christ is risen, now He's pleading,
With the father interceding,
All His vanquished foes He's leading
   In His victory.

8. Christ is risen, He's returning,
Evil forces overturning,
He'll 'catch up' all those who're yearning
   In expectancy.

9. Let us join our hearts in praising,
All our voices gladly raising,
Songs and hymns of joy thus phrasing,
   In glad psalmody.

Music © 2013 Harry Hicks
Words © 2013 Brenda Gallant

6 Christ is the only answer

Brenda Gallant

Harry Hicks

(Verse 1, under music:)
Christ is the on-ly an-swer To ev'-ry hu-man need, The au-thor of sal-va-tion, A long ac-com-plished deed. His name to sin-ners gi-ven Brings ac-cess to God's throne, An en-trance in-to hea-ven For those who are His own.

2. No other name is given
Whereby we must be saved,
No other side was riven
For sinners so depraved.
This name it gives protection,
Brings with it victory,
His glorious resurrection
Is hope for you and me.

3. Our God has spoken to us
Through Christ who is the Word,
A living demonstration
That hard hearts might be stirred.
He gives us an example,
In suffering and in love,
That we may be well fitted
To dwell with Him above.

4. And so this loving Saviour
Can give us grace to show
That henceforth our behaviour
Reveals the One we know.
Then He, Himself will bless us,
And be our great reward,
This Christ, who is the Answer;
Our ever living Lord.

Music © 2013 Harry Hicks
Words © 1986 Brenda Gallant

7 Come with gladness

Brenda Gallant
Harry Hicks

Come with gladness and rejoice,
Lift up your heart and soul and voice;
Unto us a child is born,
He the garb of flesh has worn,
Come to the earth from realms of light,
Pierced the gloom of nature's night.

2. Come with worship, come with awe,
Kneel before Him and adore.
See within that tiny child,
God and man are reconciled.
He, entwined in swaddling bands,
Holds the whole world in His hands.

3. Come with wonder as you view,
All that God has done for you.
How He stooped with wondrous grace,
And confined to time and space,
God within a human frame,
As a little baby came.

4. Come with understanding heart,
Knowing you can share a part,
On this happy Christmas day,
Homage at the manger pay.
See your God in weakness lie,
Tiny baby, born to die.

5. Come with wide enlightened eyes,
Hear the message from the skies,
Unto you is born this day
One to take your sins away.
This the Saviour, Christ the Lord,
Only true and living word.

6. Come with grief and anguish sore,
See a little babe no more,
Rather view Him lifted high,
Hanging on a cross to die.
This the reason for His birth,
Why He came from heav'n to earth.

7. Come with thankfulness and praise,
Lift your heart in joyful lays,
He who died now lives again,
King of kings for aye to reign.
Give to Him your life, your all,
At His feet in worship fall.

8. Come with expectation too,
For His promise will come true,
He will rend the clouds aside,
Claim His cleansed and waiting bride.
Work and watch and praise and pray.

Music © 2013 Harry Hicks
Words © 1992 Brenda Gallant

8   Creation

Brenda Gallant   Harry Hicks

Cre-a-tion, oh wonderful story, How God formed the earth and the sea, Revealing His power and glory Through creature and flower and tree.

2. From darkness creating the night light,
Ruled over by moon and the stars,
The sun set to measure the daylight,
And planets, like Jupiter, Mars.

3. The seas with abundance of fishes
Were ordered to stay in their place,
According to the divine wishes,
And all-seeing, infinite grace.

4. The plants, herbs and seeds were all growing,
And each was inherently good,
For God, with his foresight and knowing,
Was planning for mankind his food.

5. The birds of the air with their singing,
The creeping things after their kind,
Yet now in their order were bringing
The fellowship God wished to find.

6. So God formed a man from the earth's dust,
And gave him a garden to tend,
One who was perfect, sinless and just,
A being to treat as a friend.

7. Thus Adam appeared in perfection,
And Eve, asd a helpmate was given,
But, because of sin and rfejection,
The fellowship bond has been riven.

9   Redemption

Redemption, oh wonderful story, 'Tis ours to declare to you all, How God in His power and glory Has rescued mankind from the fall.

2. By sending His Son as our Saviour
The fellowship can be restored,
He forgives our sinful behaviour,
As promised in His Holy Word.

3. Christ took all our sins and sorrows,
As He hung there upon the cross,
Now we can have hopeful tomorrows,
And fear neither judgement or loss.

4. By rising from death in the garden,
He promises we can be free,
A personal faith brings us pardon,
For He has said "Come unto Me."

5. At this harvest time celebration
Praise the Lord for all He has done,
And there will be great jubilation,
If you turn in faith to His Son.

6. Creation shows forth all God's glory,
Perfection in all He has made,
Creation and Redemption's story,
have for us God's great love displayed.

Music © 2013 Harry Hicks
Words © 2013 Brenda Gallant

10 Emmanuel, the true expression

Brenda Gallant   Harry Hicks

(Verse 1, under music):
Emmanuel, the true expression of a heav'nly Father's love. In our hearts a deep impression: His own presence thus to prove. God with us, O wondrous story, stooping low to earth He came; From the heights of heav'nly glory to the depths of earthly shame.

2. Emmanuel - oh can you grasp it?
'tis a wonder rich and rare,
To your heart then firmly clasp it,
This great truth beyond compare.
God himself, so high and holy,
In a manger bed to lie,
Came as babe, so weak and lowly,
then, as man, to bleed and die.

3. Emmanuel - it is the reason
for this time of joy and mirth,
And to us the Christmas season
Is to celebrate the birth.
Of the One who loves us dearly
Even though we're marred by sin,
He came down to show us clearly
That our love he fain would win.

4. Emmanuel - embrace the glory
Of his wondrous love to man.
As you hear again his story,
Praise Him for redemption's plan.
Give your heart, your life an off'ring
With thanksgiving glad and true,
To the One who now is proff'ring
Everlasting life to you.

5. Emmanuel - he came to save us
By his earthly life and death.
But he'll come again to raise us,
This is what the scripture saith;
He will come again in glory,
In the twinkling of an eye,
To complete the gospel story
That will never, never die.

Music © 2013 Harry Hicks
Words © 2013 Brenda Gallant

11. Finished

Brenda Gallant — *Harry Hicks*

"Fin-ished," thought Judas, "The deed has been done, I have betrayed Him, God's dearly loved Son. "Fin-ished," said Jesus, "Now go forth and tell All the disciples, and Peter as well." Finished indeed, the price has been paid, All the world's sin on the Lamb has been laid.

2. "Finished," wept Peter,
"My Lord I've denied,
Now He will shortly
Be crucified.
Finished indeed,
My poor heart is broken,
He is denied by words I have spoken."

3. Finished, feared the ten,
And all ran away,
They loved Him dearly,
But just could not stay.
Finished indeed, their hopes were all gone,
Hadn't He really been God's only Son?

4. "Finished," said Pilate,
And called for a bowl,
"I'll now wash my hands
And cleanse my own soul;.
Finished indeed, now take him away,
You crucify Him, and have your own way."

5. "Finished," mused soldiers,
And packed up their gear,
But who is that Man
Suspended up there?
Finished indeed, His ministry o'er,
No-one to grieve but the sick and the poor.

6. "Finished," mourned Mary,
And stood 'neath the cross,
Her heart was broken,
By such a great loss.
Finished indeed, her spirit was torn,
Although 'twas for this her Son had been born.

7. "Finished," cried Jesus,
"My work is complete,
The law's just demands
My death will now meet.
Finished indeed, my work is all done,
My dying ensures the victory won."

8. "Finished," sobbed Mary,
"The sepulcre's bare,
Where have they laid Him,
Oh, tell me please, where?"
Finished indeed, no more in the tomb,
His voice is speaking to banish your gloom.

10. Finished, yes finished
the work has been done.
Praise him forever,
God's well beloved Son.
Finished indeed, salvation is free,
So lovingly wrought, for you and for me.

11. Finished oh praise Him,
The blood has been shed,
Give thanks to the one
With the thorn scarred head.
Finished indeed, yet only begun,
Let all the world praise and honour the Son.

Music © 2013 Harry Hicks
Words © 2013 Brenda Gallant

12. For those disciples

Brenda Gallant · Harry Hicks

For those dis-ci-ples long a-go, Death seemed the bit-ter end,
For they in wear-i-ness and woe Had lost their dear-est friend.

2. They had not understood His word
That he would rise again,
And when that dreadful deed occurred
It left them numb with pain.

3. But God in His Almightiness,
Did vindicate His Son,
And from the darkness of distress
Revealed a vict'ry won.

4. When Mary, blinded by her tears
And bowed with sorrow low
Gave voice to her consuming fears,
The Lord she did not know.

5. But He, in triumph, spoke her name,
Her sorrow quickly fled,
She went to spread abroad His fame:
Christ risen from the dead!

6. "I go a-fishing," Peter said,
And others joined him too.
Their lives were empty, purpose dead,
They knew not what to do.

7. But Jesus stood upon the shore,
Inviting them to dine,
Then, soothing Peter's heart so sore,
Revealed His great design.

8. A recommission he received,
And then the Spirit's dower,
Now all who have in Christ believed,
Can know that selfsame power.

Music © 2013 Harry Hicks
Words © 1986 Brenda Gallant

13 Go forth

Brenda Gallant   Harry Hicks

Fear not the fu-ture, it is in God's hands,
Go where he bids you, fol-low His com-mands,
Strength will be giv-en what-ev-er life de-mands;
Go forth, go forth, go forth.

2. God's way is perfect, make it your delight,
For you are precious in His holy sight,
Follow His leading, walking in His light,
   Go forth, go forth, go forth.

3. Lean on His promise, take it to your heart,
He will be with you now you've made a start,
Just trust Him fully, He will do His part,
   Believe, believe, believe.

4. Go then with blessings ringing in your ears,
His promises alleviate your fears,
Take with you love and our continuing prayers,
   Good, goodbye, goodbye.

Music © 2013 Harry Hicks
Words © 2013 Brenda Gallant

14 God loved the world

Brenda Gallant
Harry Hicks

God loved the world but sorely grieved, That men his love had spurned, Their hearts by sin had been deceived, To their own ways they turned.

2. The Son of God came down to earth,
He left His throne above,
He came to give us second birth,
And show His Father's love.

3. He came to seek and save the lost,
To give them inward peace,
But oh, with what an awful cost,
He paid for their release!

4. This heavenly peace is free to all
Who on His name believe.
Oh, have you heard the Saviour's call?
Will you His peace receive?

5. He'll give you joy from day to day,
His presence you will know,
No matter what may come your way,
The Lord will see you through.

6. No fear in life, no fear in death,
With Christ your dearest friend,
For He who grants you daily breath,
Is with you to the end.

7. Then praise Him for His love and grace,
Rest sweetly in His care,
Until, one day, you see His face,
Eternity to share.

Music © 2013 Harry Hicks
Words © 1986 Brenda Gallant

15 He shows His love

Brenda Gallant
Harry Hicks

(Verse 1)
God shows His love and glory
In ev'ry-thing we see,
The oft repeated story
In ev'ry flower and tree.
The gran-deur of the moun-tains,
The splen-dour of the lake,
The spark-ling water foun-tains
Reveal Him for our sake.

2. God shows himself unwilling
That even one be lost,
The whole creation filling
And with His seal embossed.
Thus He revealed the mystery
Of creatorial power,
And spoke, throughout all history
Until this very hour.

3. But God again, has spoken
Through His beloved Son,
That those whom sin has broken
From Satan's power be won.
This perfect revelation
Is ours to recognise,
Accept the free salvation
And press toward the skies.

4. Oh, have you heard Him speaking
Through Jeus Christ, the lord,
For He is ever seeking
Those who will heed His word.
He gives the invitation;
"Come unto me, and rest."
Through trial and tribulation,
In Him you will be blest.

Music © 2013 Harry Hicks
Words © 2013 Brenda Gallant

16 God's promise

Brenda Gallant

Harry Hicks

God's pro-mise now has been ful-filled, His Son in flesh ap-pears, The One whose com-ing was fore-told Down through the pass-ing years.

2. He came to bruise the serpent's head,
To triumph over sin,
To bridge the gap twixt man and God,
And let the sinner in.

3. The angels plainly gave the news
"To you this day is born,"
But sadly some reject the love
So freely giv'n and shown.

4. "No room" was heard, when, long ago
God needed place to stay,
An outcast in a stable bare,
Rejected, in the hay.

5. But there were those who saw the light,
And eager to obey,
They went with haste and found the child,
And worshipped where he lay.

6. They left the stable full of joy
To spread the news abroad,
Their lives were changed because they knew
Christ, their incarnate Lord.

7. Beyond the cradle looms the cross,
It's message plain for all,
Atonement for mankind was planned
Before man's dreadful fall.

8. His birth, His life, His death were all
To save us from our sin,
Look unto Him and be ye saved;
Invite the Saviour in!

9. Without Him life is lived in vain,
He came to be the Way,
His second Advent soon will come,
Be ready for that day!

Music © 2013 Harry Hicks
Words © 2013 Brenda Gallant

17 God's Spirit

Brenda Gallant
Harry Hicks

God's Spi-rit speak-ing through His Word Is in our midst to - night,
And when His voice is tru - ly heard Dark - ness and sin take flight.

2. He speaks because he loves you so,
And craves you for His own,
Such love that made His heart o'erflow
To make a cross His throne.

3. The Spirit takes the things of Christ
And makes them real to you,
He shows you that His death sufficed,
There's nothing more to do.

4. "If you have ears, then let them hear,"
Our Lord said long ago,
His message sounds forever clear
That you His peace might know.

5. Will you then heed His loving voice,
Confess your sin and woe,
Wholeheartedly make Him your choice
As to His cross you go.

6. Then onward into life anew,
His Spirit in your heart,
Say "Lord, what Thou wilt have me do,
And give me grace to start."

Music © 2013 Harry Hicks
Words © 1985 Brenda Gallant

18   In the beginning

Brenda Gallant   Harry Hicks

In the beginning was the Word, The Word was with our God.
By His own voice creation stirred Where foot had never trod.

2. In Him was life, in Him was light,
The light for every man,
Because He knew the sinner's plight
He wrought salvation's plan.

3. He came unto His own, but they
Received Him not, we're told,
they turned their hearts from him away;
Remained outside the fold.

4. But those who did the word receive,
the sons of God became,
this is for all who will believe
In that most precious name.

5. The Word made flesh, among us dwelt,
His glory to behold,
Then let that word our hard hearts melt,
As in the days of old.

6. His glory, full of truth and grace,
Is ours this Christmas time,
We see, reflected in Christ's face
The heights of love sublime.

7. This wondrous mystery we declare
To all who will take heed,
That in the fulness we may share,
And then be blessed indeed.

Music © 2013 Harry Hicks
Words © 2013 Brenda Gallant

19 Is it well?

Brenda Gallant
Harry Hicks

Lyrics under music: Is it well with thy soul? Is it well with thy soul? Can you say 'It is well with my soul?' Jesus died on the tree, Purchased pardon for thee, Can you say 'It is well with my soul'? Yes, it is well, I know it is well, Precious blood for my cleansing, What a story to tell!

2. Is it well in thy life,
Is it well in thy life,
Are you living in His victory,
In the toil and the strife,
Is it well in thy life,
Is there peace and His sweet harmony?
   Yes it is well,
   I know it is well,
   His power worketh in me,
   All temptation to quell.

3. Is it well in thy home,
Is it well in thy home,
Is Christ in control over all?
Problems great, problems small,
Does he deal with them all,
Is it well, is it well in thy home?
   Yes it is well,
   I know it is well,
   For Christ is my Captain,
   And with me He doth dwell.

4. Now the Bible is true,
Has a message for you,
It calls you to faith in the lord.
Do be sure you are right,
For a terrible plight
Awaits those who turn from the Word.
   Will you believe?
   And His promise receive,
   Are you trusting in Jesus
   Unto Him will you cleave?

Music © 2013 Harry Hicks
Words © 2013 Brenda Gallant

20. Let me tell you/Wonderful place

Brenda Gallant
Harry Hicks

(1st Soloist?) Let me tell you to-night, Of the man-sions so bright, That the sav-iour has gone to pre-pare, There's no sick-ness or night, Faith is turned in-to sight, And the glo-ry at last we will share. (2nd Soloist?) Won-der-ful place, Where we see our Lord's face, There to praise Him and thank Him For His soul sav-ing grace.

2. Let me tell you tonight
Of the wonderful sight,
That the shepherds of old went to view,
God incarnate on earth,
A miraculous birth,
And the best thing of all: it is true!
  God came to earth
  A miraculous birth
By His coming revealing
Just how much you are worth.

3. Let me tell you tonight,
Of the sinner's sad plight,
And the God who was willing to die,
How He went to the cross,
Suffered anguish and loss
To bring rebels and sinners both nigh.
  Look to the tree,
  Jesus died there for thee,
Bore your sin in His body,
That your soul might go free.

4. Let me tell you tonight
Of the glorious sight,
There's a tomb with the stone rolled away,
For the Saviour arose,
Having vanquished His foes,
resurrection, Oh glorious day!
  Now He's on high
  Having once come to die
Seated there in the glory
Bidding us to come nigh.

5. Let me tell you tonight,
He will burst into sight
When He comes in the clouds by and by.
Have your sins been forgiven?
Are you ready for heaven?
Once there; never a tear or a sigh.
  Wonderful place,
  Where we see our Lord's face,
There to praise Him and thank Him
For His soul-saving grace.

Music © 2013 Harry Hicks
Words © 1993 Brenda Gallant

21 Long, long ago

Brenda Gallant　　　　　　　　　　　　　　　　　　Harry Hicks

Long, long a-go God sent His Son, To save man-kind from sin, He tru-ly is the on-ly One, By whom we en-ter in.

2. "I am the door," the Saviour said,
No other entrance giv'n,
He banishes all fear and dread,
And makes us fit for Heav'n.

3. Then enter in by that blest door,
Don't try another way,
With Him to dwell for evermore,
In realms of endless day.

Music © 2013 Harry Hicks
Words © 2013 Brenda Gallant

22 Long, long ago

Brenda Gallant · Harry Hicks

(Lyrics under music:)
Long, long a-go, God made a pro-mise true; Though men had sinned, the gos-pel light shone through. The wo-man's seed would bruise the ser-pent's head, The sin-less One would suf-fer in man's stead. Down through the years the pro-phets oft fore-told God's lov-ing mes-sage that will not grow old.

2. This message brought a note of joy and peace,
Promised to captives freedom and release
Of victory o'er sin and death and hell,
This is the good news Christmas has to tell.
Thus in the fulness of God's time He came,
Our lovely Saviour, Jesus is His name.

3. See, now He lies in that crude bed of straw,
While from the skies the angel voices pour,
Proclaiming to the dark and slumbering world,
That now, at last, God's message in unfurled.
Peace on the earth, goodwill to sinful man,
Promised fulfillment of redemption's plan.

4. Now, look again, with wide and wondering eyes,
See, on a cross the anguished Saviour dies.
He who was born to suffer in man's stead,
Now feels the wrath of God upon His head,
He bears our sins, this sinless Son of God,
Who in the form of man this planet trod.

5. With eyes of faith then let us all behold
The One whose life and death were all foretold.
Look past the manger and the mournful tomb,
See, resurrection light has pieced the gloom.
One day He's coming back to earth to reign
The second advent - let's take up the strain!

6. Glory to God, the Father and the Son,
The Holy Spirit, blessed Three in One!
This Christmastide give praise to God alone,
Invite Him in and let Him take the throne.
Make Him your King and crown Him Lord of all,
In glad surrender at His feet to fall.

Music © 2013 Harry Hicks
Words © 2013 Brenda Gallant

23 Jove - Joy - Peace

Brenda Gallant
Harry Hicks

Have you love in your heart That will ne-ver de-part, No mat-ter how tes-ted and tried, Is the Lord all in all, Have you heard His love call, "For you, help-less sin-ner I died." He gave His love Sa-tan's fet-ters to move, And now He is liv-ing His re-demp-tion to prove.

2. Have you joy in your heart
That will never depart
No matter what sorrows sweep o'er,
Only His joy will stay
When your sky seems all grey
And earth's trifles attract you no more.
   He is your joy
   And your life will employ
   To show forth His praises
   And the tempter destroy.

3. Have you peace in your heart
That will never depart
No matter what trials may come,
Is the Lord in control
And is heaven your goal,
That blessed, eternal, bright home.
   He is your peace,
   He can give you release,
   His arm will support you,
   And His love never cease.

Music © 2013 Harry Hicks
Words © 2013 Brenda Gallant

24 Mary and Joseph

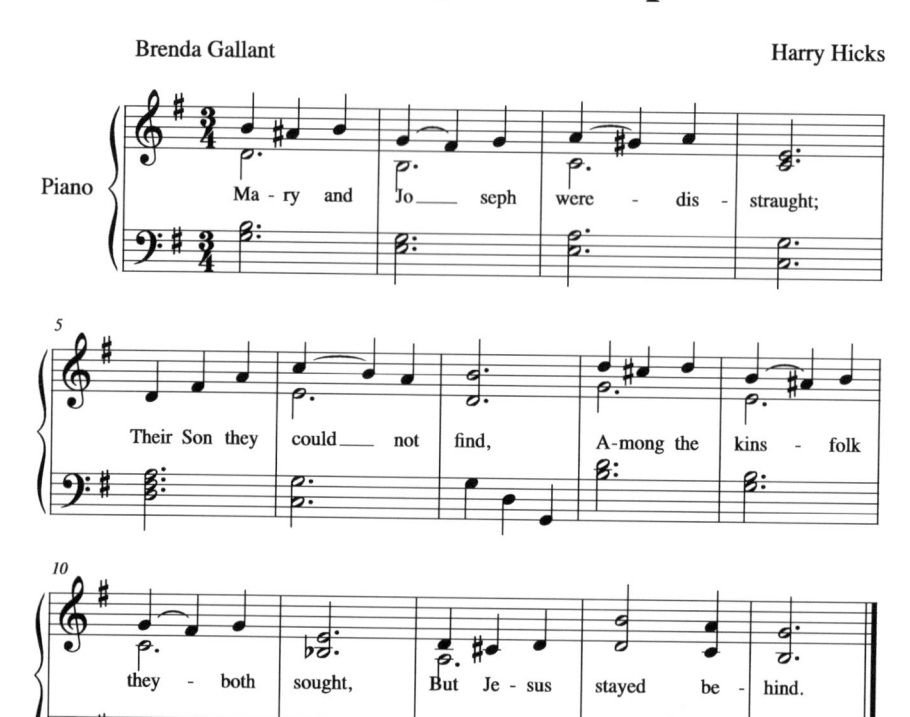

Brenda Gallant Harry Hicks

Ma-ry and Jo___ seph were - dis - straught;
Their Son they could___ not find, A-mong the kins - folk
they - both sought, But Je - sus stayed be - hind.

2. They has assumed that He was there,
As they had journeyed on.
Now to their grief and deep dispair
they found they were alone.

3. Back to the temple they both went,
And there they found their Son,
The One whom God had to them sent,
But not to them alone.

4. For Mary's Son, is God come down
To save mankind from sin,
And he can be your very own,
If you will let Him in.

5. Don't journey on without the Lord;
You need Him by your side,
For He has promised in His word,
To be your friend and guide.

Music © 2013 Harry Hicks
Words © 2013 Brenda Gallant

25 No other way

Brenda Gallant   Harry Hicks

Oh hearken now to God's own Word
This message come to you,
Down through the years it has been heard,
Ancient, yet ever new.

2. No other way to get to heav'n,
No matter what men say,
Only the one that had been giv'en
Jesus, Himself, the Way.

3. No other truth on which to rest,
For Christ alone is true,
God's promises have stood the test,
So you may trust Him too.

4. No other life can e'er compare
What what Christ offers you,
He is the life and you may share
In all its blessings too.

5. No other name can meet your need,
Jesus alone will save,
This warning message you must heed,
So solemn and so grave.

6. Oh follow Him who is the Way,
Trust Him, so wise and true,
Give Him your life as from today
And he will live in you.

7. Take Jesus as your Saviour now,
He'll cleanse you from your sin,
Before His Kingship gladly bow
And let Him reign within.

8. Then bear that blessed holy name
With deep humility,
And live to spread abroad His fame
Wherever you may be.

Music © 2013 Harry Hicks
Words © 2013 Brenda Gallant

26 Oh flee

Brenda Gallant Harry Hicks

(Verse 1 lyrics under music): Oh flee as a bird to the moun-tain, Frtom God's wrath that is sure-ly your due, Oh, wash in that still flow-ing foun-tain, That foun-tain was o-pened for you - That foun-tain is o-pen for you, That foun-tain is o-pen for you, Oh, flee as a bird to the moun-tain, That foun-tain is o-pen for you.

2. There's refuge and shelter in Jesus,
He died that you might enter in,
For He is the Rock of Salvation,
The answer to all of your sin.

Chorus:
**That fountain is open for you,
That fountain is open for you,
Oh, flee as a bird to the mountain,
That fountain is open for you.**

3. There's refuge and shelter in Jesus,
Enough to supply every need,
He offers you cleansing and pardon,
And guidance if you let Him lead.
That fountain.......

4. There's refuge and shelter in Jesus,
For time and eternity too,
That wonderful, infinite mercy,
Sufficient to see you right through.
That fountain.....

5. There's refuge and shelter in Jesus,
He died and is living again,
One day He will come back to take you,
Triumphant for ever to reign.
That fountain....

Music © 2013 Harry Hicks
Words © 2013 Brenda Gallant

27 Oh who is this

Brenda Gallant
Harry Hicks

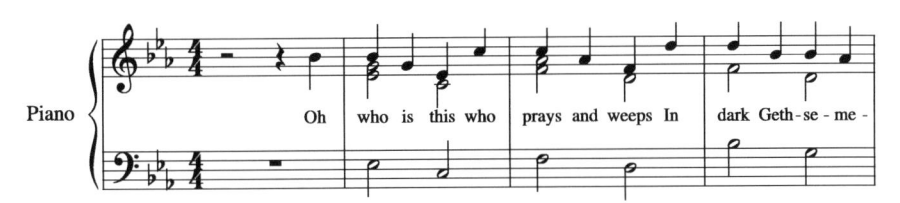

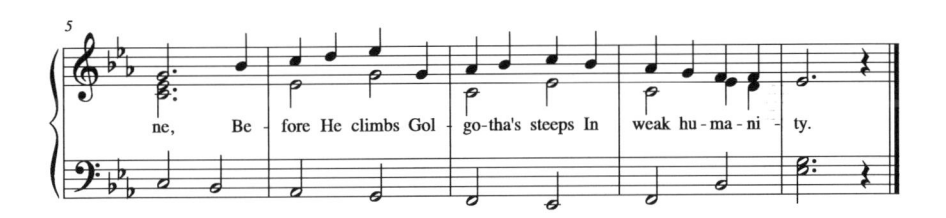

Oh who is this who prays and weeps In dark Gethsemene, Before He climbs Golgotha's steeps In weak humanity.

2. Just see him now, as bending low
He wrestles long in prayer,
With drops of blood upon His brow
He agonises there.

3. The battle fought is hardly won,
He bows himself to bear,
Redemption's work at last begun
For all mankind to share.

4. Oh who is this in robes arrayed
And with a thorny crown?
Forsaken, mocked, by friend betrayed,
With pain and grief weighed down.

5. Oh who is this, his visage marred,
Condemned at last to die?
His hands and feet with nail prints scarred,
As He is lifted high.

6. He hangs in shame twixt earth and sky,
Abused and sore reviled,
That man to God might be brought nigh,
Forever reconciled.

7. Oh who is this in linen shroud,
Now numbered with the dead?
To take God's wrath He meekly bowed,
And suffered in our stead.

8. It is the Lord, it is the Lord,
He burst from sin's dread chains!
The living and exalted Word,
Once more in heaven reigns.

9. Oh have you seen the risen Christ,
Low at His feet to fall,
His sacrifice for sin sufficed,
Now yield to Him your all.

10. One day He's coming back again,
To call to Him His own,
This message echoes loud and plain,
And should be widely known.

11. Will you be ready for that day,
Whenever that may be,
Oh do not trust to anything,
But galdy bow the knee.

Music © 2013 Harry Hicks
Words © 1992 Brenda Gallant

28 Our Saviour

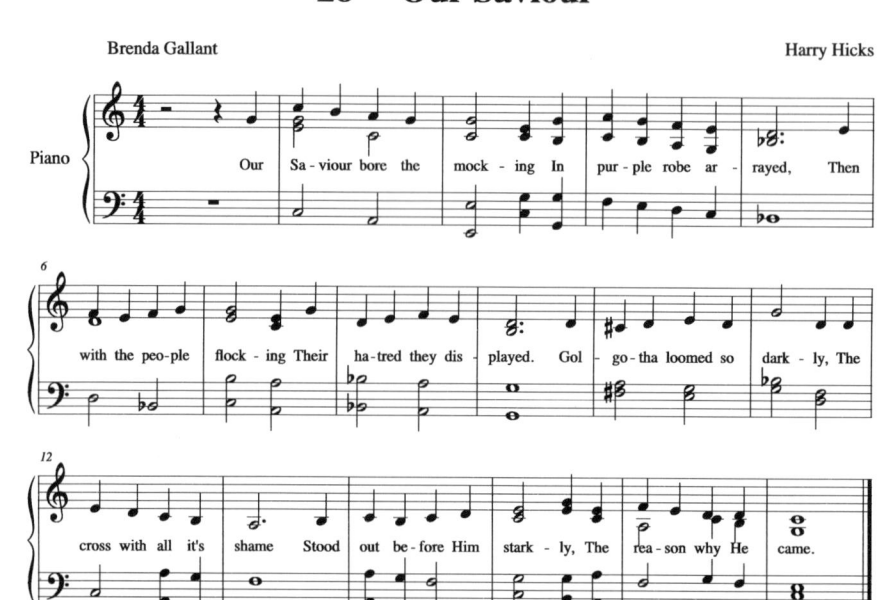

Brenda Gallant / Harry Hicks

Our Saviour bore the mocking In purple robe arrayed, Then with the people flocking Their hatred they displayed. Golgotha loomed so darkly, The cross with all it's shame Stood out before Him starkly, The reason why He came.

2. Then myrrh and wine they proffered,
A cup He would not drink,
But His own self He offered,
From suff'ring did not shrink.
They crucified the Saviour,
Then gambled by His cross,
Suich ignorant behaviour
To their eternal loss.

3. The superscription written
Proclaimed the King of Jews,
The sinless One was smitten,
His life to gladly lose.
In order to save others,
Himself He would not save,
He died to make men brothers,
And triumph o'er the grave.

4. Then as He hung suspended
Betwixt the earth and sky,
The daylight swift was ended
When Jesus bowed to die.
He felt himslf forsaken
By God in that dread hour,
The temple court was shaken
By His almighty power.

5. This man was truly God's Son,
One watching Him then cried,
And now with that dread deed done,
It could not be denied.
Those standing by observing
Acknowledged God, made man,
And we, though undeserving
Are part of His great plan.

Music © 2013 Harry Hicks
Words © 1986 Brenda Gallant

29 Praise the God of truth and love

Brenda Gallant
Harry Hicks

Lyrics under music: Praise the God of truth and love — Lifted high. He who stoops from heav'n above — Draws us nigh. See the beauty all around, Miracles of skill abound, All creation joins the sound — Give Him praise.

2. Mark the beauty of the skies, Gaze in awe.
View the stars with wondering eyes And adore
   See the everlasting hills,
   Note the sparkling fountain rills,
   Hear how all creation thrills,
     Give Him praise.

3. God's creation shouts His name, Clear and plain.
Far and wide it spreads his fame, And again.
   All mankind can hear His voice
   he has given each the choice,
   To believe Him and rejoice,
     Give Him praise.

4. "What is man,' the psalmist cried, Long ago.
Overcome with awe he tried God to know.
   All creation speaks His worth
   Azure skies and friendly earth,
   These all set the Godhead forth
     Give him praise.

5. These all speak, their voices one, Of His might.
But he speaks now through His son; His delight.
   He who left the heav'n above,
   Object of His Father's love,
   Comes our sin and guilt to move,
     Give Him praise.

6. Jesus Christ surpasses all, He will save.
All the souls who on Him call Life shall have.
   He who died and rose again
   Brings salvation in His train
   Let each heart take up the strain,
     Give Him praise.

Music © 2013 Harry Hicks
Words © 1989 Brenda Gallant

30 Seek

Brenda Gallant / Harry Hicks

Seek, oh seek the Lord-of-Glory, While He may be found,
Heed redemption's wondrous story, Hear the joyful sound;
Seek ye, seek ye, Turn unto the Lord,
Hear the loving exhortation In the precious Word.

2. Call upon the Lord of Glory,
While He still is near,
Throw yourself upon His mercy,
There is nought to fear.
    Call ye, call ye,
    While the Lord is near,
    Take the living invitation;
    Love that casts out fear.

3. Forsake, forsake all your own way,
And unrighteous thought,
For the Lord will truly welcome
One He long has sought.
    Forsake ye, forsake ye,
    Turn from your own way,
    God is willing to receive thee;
    Come to Him today.

4. Return to God, who then will pardon,
More abundantly,
Do not let your spirit harden,
Come, He calls for thee.
    Return ye, return ye,
    Return unto the Lord,
    He is waiting to receive thee,
    Welcome is assured.

Music © 2013 Harry Hicks
Words © 2013 Brenda Gallant

31 Slumbering in a manger

Brenda Gallant
Harry Hicks

Slumb'-ring in a man-ger, Ho-ly, meek, and un-de-filed, All the God-head cap-tured, In a ti-ny new-born child.

2. Watching on the hillside,
Humble shepherds hear the word,
Spoken by the angels
A Saviour, which is Chfrist the Lord.

3. Travelling from the east land,
Come the watchers of the sky,
Following the Natal star,
Of the baby born to die.

4. Pondering the mystery,
Mary tends the infant lord,
Promised by the angel,
God made flesh, the living Word.

5. Shepherds bow in homage,
Wise men bring their gifts of worth
To their God incarnate,
He who came from heaven to earth.

6. Ah, we must not linger,
By the manger and the hay,
For the Lord our Saviour,
Came to bear orur sins away.

7. We must view Him hanging
Bearing all our sin and loss,
Gone the rustic manger,
Now a cursed RToman cross.

8. This the wondrous reason
Why we celebrate today,
He has paid the ransome,
He has borne our sins away.

9. Past the lowly manger,
Gone the anguish of the tree,
For our Lord now reigneth
In pow'er and majesty.

10. Come we then to worship,
Bring our hearts, our lives, our all,
Praise Him and adore him,
At His feet in wonder fall.

Music © 2013 Harry Hicks
Words © 2013 Brenda Gallant

32 The light

Brenda Gallant   Harry Hicks

When Christ was born, God used a star To show to all His birth, And wise men travelled from afar, Acknowleging His worth.

2. That star was there to be a guide,
To shed abroad the light,
A radiance spreading far and wide,
Unveiled to human sight.

3. Jesus, Himself, is that true light,
And all who follow Him,
Will find their darkness turned to sight,
A sight that grows not dim.

4. Come to the Light, and let Him shine
Into your sinful heart,
Yield to that radiance, all divine,
Christ will Himself impart.

Music © 2013 Harry Hicks
Words © 2013 Brenda Gallant

33 The Lord is here

Brenda Gallant
Harry Hicks

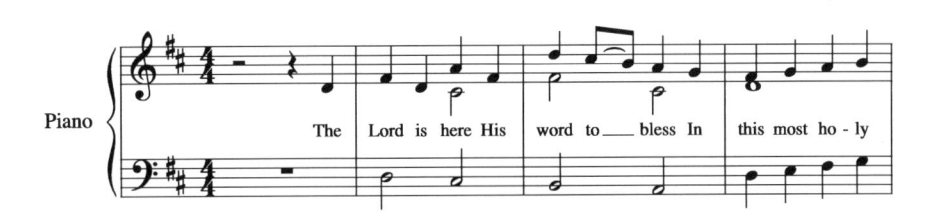

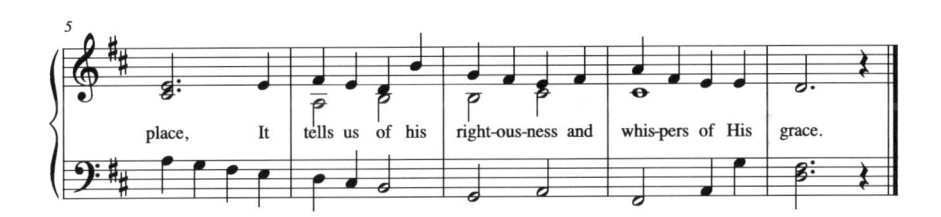

The Lord is here His word to bless In this most ho-ly place, It tells us of his right-ous-ness and whis-pers of His grace.

2. The Lord is here, he sees your need
Just as in the days of old,
And unto all who will take heed
He will His love unfold.

3. The Lord is here, He knows your sin,
But loves you just the same,
He wants to cleanse your heart within,
Through faith in His dear name.

4. The Lord is love in all His power,
To strengthen and to heal,
Oh hear his voice this very hour,
And tell Him how you feel.

5. The Lord is here, your soul to save,
It was for you He died,
To save you from a hopeless grave
God's Son was crucified.

6. The Lord is here, the price is paid,
More precious still than gold,
Accept the sacrifice he made
To win you for His fold.

7. Arise and go with grateful heart,
Trusting in Christ alone,
He'll make you whole in every part,
Your life shall be His throne.

Music © 2013 Harry Hicks
Words © 2013 Brenda Gallant

34 The Manger

Brenda Gallant / Harry Hicks

He lay in a manger, 'Twas gi-ven to Him, That poor lit-tle stran-ger, In sta-ble so dim. In great con-de-sen-tion That One from on high Should leave His great man-sion, And come here to die.

2. That baby so tender,
So humble and meek,
Left heaven's sheer splendour,
Our lost souls to seek.
Tha manger that held Him,
And gave Him repose,
He exchanged for a cross,
Nailed there by His foes.

3. Now ris'n and victorious,
And seated on high,
Our Saviour all glorious,
Desires to draw nigh,
But not as a stranger,
Unloved and unknown,
Your heart, not a manger,
Should be His blest throne.

Music © 2013 Harry Hicks
Words © 2013 Brenda Gallant

35 The Saviour Christ

Brenda Gallant
Harry Hicks

The Sav-iour Christ left heav'n a-bove And came to this poor earth To show us all His Fath-er's love, and of-fer us new birth.

2. He came right down to reach the lost,
To bear the shame and sin;
Salvation at tremendous cost
That He your love might win.

3. Oh, have you glimpsed Him hanging there
Upon that awful tree,
And can you feel His tender care,
Who died, to make you free.

4. Tonight He speaks through His own Word,
To those who will take heed,
And if His voice is truly heard,
He'll meet the deepest need.

5. So come to Him and do not wait,
He'll make your heart His home,
Tomorrow may be just too late,
Oh, hear Him pleading "Come."

Music © 2013 Harry Hicks
Words © 1986 Brenda Gallant

36 The happy Christmas Day

Brenda Gallant
Harry Hicks

On this happy Christmas day, Tune your hearts in joyful lay, Praise the Father and the Son, With the Spirit, Three in One. God's great promise has come true, Gospel grace is shining through.

2. Like the shepherds long ago,
May we to the manger go,
See the Infant lying there,
Our humanity to share.
See Him as the promised One,
God's beloved only Son.

3. Long ago God gave His Word,
And the hearts of men were stirred,
For One promised at the fall
Would release from sins entrall.
The Messiah soon would come,
God's beloved only Son.

4. Thus it was that Jesus came,
Though men scorned His precious Name,
As a little Babe was born
In a stable all forlorn.
When He came to this poor earth
Very few perceived His worth.

5. Only shepherds went to see
At His manger bowed the knee,
And the wise men travelled far,
Following His natal star.
These rejoiced and spread abroad
All that they had seen and heard.

6. When He grew to be a man,
He fulfilled the Father's plan,
Chose to suffer in our stead,
On the cross He hung and bled.
Jesus died our souls to save,
Rose in triumph o'er the grave.

7. That first Advent showed God's face,
Ushered in this day of grace.
May we give Him all our love,
He who left the heav'n above,
Welcome Him with hearts aglow;
Live for Him while here below.

Music © 2013 Harry Hicks
Words © 1994 Brenda Gallant

37 Upon the cross

Brenda Gallant
Harry Hicks

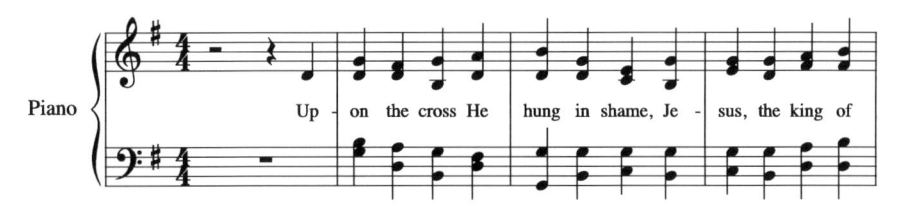

Up - on the cross He hung in shame, Je - sus, the king of Jews, They vain-ly ar - gue o'er His name, His King-ship they re - fuse.

2. Then for His raiment soldiers played,
That Scripture be fulfilled,
On earthly gain their minds were stayed,
The Prince of Life they killed.

3. His mother, Mary, standing there,
Watching His pain and woe,
Heard Him commit her to the care
Of one who loved him so.

4. God's Word was once again fulfilled,
"I thirst" they heard Him cry,
A sponge with vinegar was filled,
To give Him e'er He die.

5. Then "It is finished" Jesus said,
And bound His head and died.
He gave His life in sinners' stead
When He was crucified.

6. None of His bones were broken, that
More Scripture be fulfilled,
But when with spear they pierced His side,
Water and blood was spilled.

7. This is the record and it's true,
Giv'n that we might believe,
Salvation freely offered to
All who His love receive.

8. Look on this pierced form and see
His heart of selfless love,
Trust Him for all eternity,
He, who now reigns above.

Music © 2013 Harry Hicks
Words © 1984 Brenda Gallant

38 Watching, waiting

Brenda Gallant　　　　　　　　　　　　　　　　　Harry Hicks

Watch-ing, wait-ing for the Lord, As re-vealed in God's own word.
Si-me-on was rea-dy, when God, in Christ, ap-peared to men.

2. When the parents brought the child,
Lowly infant, meek and mild.
He was recognised by one
Long prepared for God's dear Son.

3. Open arms received with joy
Mary's little baby boy,
God's own promise had come true,
Gopspel light was shining through.

4. Anna, too, had waited long
For the One to right all wrong,
She gave thanks with grateful heart,
In His story shares a part.

5. Have you recognised God's Son
As the true and only One,
Who can take away your sin
If you will invite Him in.

6. Be like those who in the past
Both received Messiah at last.
Lifted hearts with praise above,
Thanking God for His great love.

Music © 2013 Harry Hicks
Words © 2013 Brenda Gallant

39   We thank Thee

Brenda Gallant   Harry Hicks

We thank Thee for Thy presence, Lord, As promised in Thy Word, Forever be Thy name adored, Thy voice be truly heard.

2. We thank Thee for Thy wondrous grace,
Thy love, immense and free,
Extended to our sinful race,
To draw us, Lord, to Thee.

3. We thank Thee, Lord, that Thou dost speak
And move from heart to heart,
The sinful, restless souls to seek,
Forgiveness to impart.

4. We pray Thee, Lord, Thy truth to take,
In Holy Spirit power,
And as our lives Thine imprint make,
As from this very hour.

4. We pray Thee that Thy still small voice
Will penetrate the soul,
That many here will make the choice,
By Thee to be made whole.

6. This prayer, we offer, Lord, to Thee,
Move in our midst we pray,
Cause seeking ones to be set free,
Oh, let them come today.

Music © 2013 Harry Hicks
Words © 1989 Brenda Gallant

40. What a wonderful salvation

Brenda Gallant / Harry Hicks

Verse 1 (with music):
What a wonderful salvation! We are priv'ledged to proclaim,
From the heart of God the Father, And His blessed Son who came.
On the cruel cross suspended Christ Himself bore all your sin,
There that spotless life was ended So that you might enter in.

2. What a wonderful salvation!
Purchased for you long ago,
By the death of Christ the Saviour,
That forgiveness you may know.
   For your sin, though red like crimson,
   Can be whiter than the snow,
   You can flee to Him for refuge,
   Peace and safety you can know.

3. What a wonderful salvation!
Freely by God's grace supplied,
Offered to you by the Saviour,
Who has suffered, bled, and died.
   By His death and resurrection
   You can full salvation know,
   For His blood is your protection,
   If you plunge beneath that flow.

4. What a wonderful salvation!
Have you made it all your own?
Are you trusting in God's mercy,
Which, in Christ, is fully shown!
   God, Himself will be your refuge,
   He's a strong and mighty tower,
   He will shelter and protect you,
   By His own almighty power.

Music © 2013 Harry Hicks
Words © 2013 Brenda Gallant

41 When the Lord

Brenda Gallant

Harry Hicks

Piano

8ves in the bass

When the Lord shall come in pow'r, In that bles-sed un-known hour, Will you be 'caught up' with Him, Where the light will not grow dim? Are you look-ing day by day, When He comes with-out de-lay? Trump shall sound, arch-an-gel voice, Sin-ner, have you made your choice?

2. Living in this day of grace,
You can humbly seek His face,
Turn from sin and trust His love,
He will then all guilt remove.
   He will wash your sins away,
   Heed what Holy Scriptures say,
   Jesus calls - "Come unto Me,
   Find salvation full and free."

Music © 2013 Harry Hicks
Words © 2013 Brenda Gallant

42 Where is He?

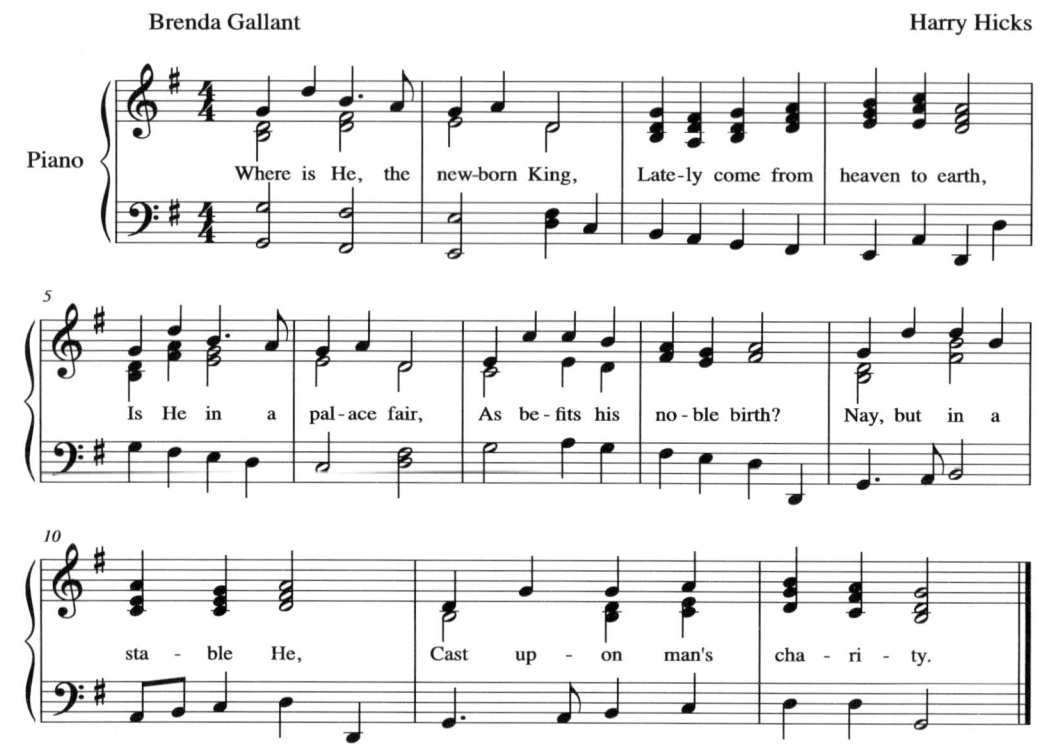

Brenda Gallant — Harry Hicks

Verse 1 (music): Where is He, the new-born King, Lately come from heaven to earth, Is He in a palace fair, As befits his noble birth? Nay, but in a stable He, Cast upon man's charity.

2. Where is he, the infant Lord,
Maker of the earth and skies,
Is He in a downy bed,
God come down in human guise?
No, but in a manger bare
With the cattle thus to share.

3. Where is he, the Saviour King,
Heralded by angels bright?
Hurriedly the shepherds go
To see the amazing sight.
Kingly robes are laid aside,
Human form now dignified.

4. Where is he, born King of Jews?
Wise men from the east inquired,
Travelled to Jerusalem
To give homage they desired.
Found Him in a humble town,
At his feet they bowed them down.

5. Where is he? the Son of Man
As he heals the sick and sad,
Cheering sin benighted lives,
Bringing joy and making glad.
He is lost among the crowd
As they clamour long and loud.

6. Where is he? In Pilate's hall,
Lone, despised and cast aside,
Buffeted and spat upon
"Crucify Him," they have cried,
Now He hangs upon a cross,
Bearing all our sin and loss.

7. Where is he? Cold in the tomb,
Carried there by caring friends,
Gently laid at last to rest,
Thus his earthly life he ends.
Soldiers seal and guard the grave,
Christ, who died our souls to save.

8. Where is he? The tomb is bare,
Death is vanquished once for all!
Christ has triumphed over death,
He will save all those who call.
Now he reigns once more above,
Object of His Father's love.

9. Where is he? This Christmas time,
as we celebrate His birth,
Is he present in your home,
Have you recognised His worth?
Or is He still left outside,
Spurned by those for whom He died.

10. Where is he? Enthroned on high,
Worshipped by the hosts above,
He who stooped to bring us nigh,
Now desires our lives, our love,
He will come to earth again;
Crown Him King, and let Him reign!

Music © 2013 Harry Hicks
Words © 2013 Brenda Gallant

43 Where oh where

Brenda Gallant

Harry Hicks

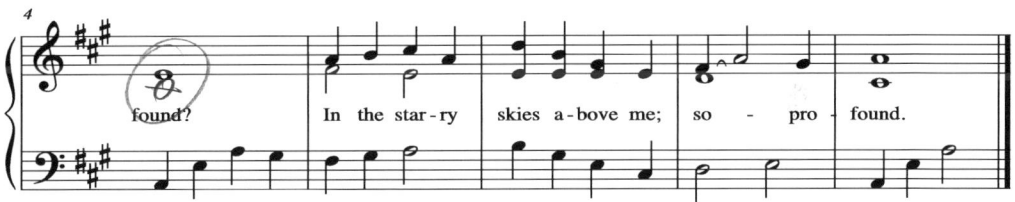

Where oh where may I behold Him, Where can he be found? In the star-ry skies a-bove me; so pro-found.

2. Where oh where may I behold Him,
In the ocean deep?
All it's waves and all it's billows
Bounds must keep.

3. Where oh where may I behold Him
In the forest green?
All the waving branches witness
Pow'r unseen.

4. Where oh where may I behold Him?
On a lonely hill,
Hanging on a cross suspended,
Cold and still.

5. Where oh where may I behold Him?
In a borrowed grave,
He who came to earth from heaven
Just to save.

6. Where oh where may I behold Him?
Risen from the tomb,
By His rising He has banished
Fear and gloom.

7. Where oh where may I behold Him?
In the glory now,
Unto Him who died to save us
We must bow.

8. If you truly want to find Him,
You must seek His face,
He will save and keep you always
By His grace.

Music © 2013 Harry Hicks
Words © 2013 Brenda Gallant

44 Why seek the living

Brenda Gallant

Harry Hicks

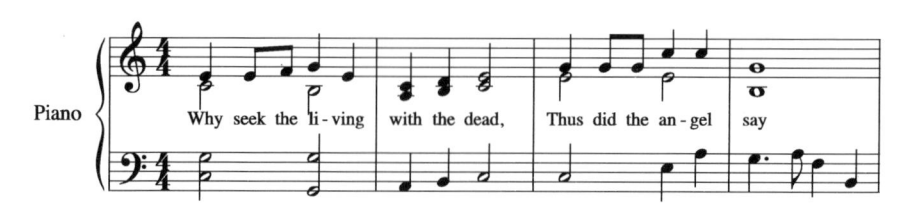

[Musical score with lyrics: "Why seek the li-ving with the dead, Thus did the an-gel say To wo-men, as sad tears they shed On re-sur-rec-tion day."]

2. The tomb is bare, the body gone,
The Saviour lives to save,
Into the hearts the glory shone,
And sweet assurance gave.

3. They then remembered His own word,
That he would rise again,
The glorious news their sad hearts stirred,
Erasing all the pain.

4. They went with joy, the news to spread
That their beloved Lord
Had ris'n triumphant from the dead;
The ever-living Word.

5. Oh, have you viewed the empty grave,
And seen the empty cross?
For Jesus died your soul to save
From death and certain loss.

6. Now at the dawn of this new year,
Be sure you seek and find
The One who casteth out all fear;
So loving, good and kind.

7. He will forgive and cleanse from sin,
And live within your heart,
If you will only ask Him in:
Now is the time to start.

Music © 2013 Harry Hicks
Words © 2013 Brenda Gallant

45 Your God is here

Brenda Gallant　　　　　　　　　　　　　　　　Harry Hicks

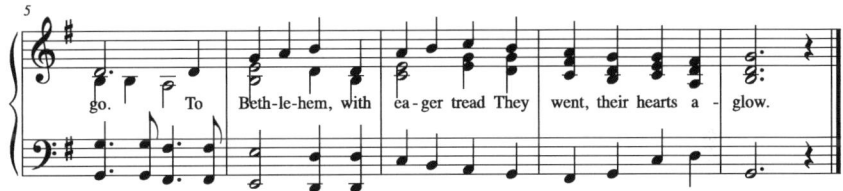

Your God is here, the angel said To shepherds long ago. To Bethlehem, with eager tread They went, their hearts aglow.

2. Your God is here, in manger bare
Where cattle once were fed,
His mother laid Him gently there,
To rest His infant head.

3. Your God is here, in humble home,
The wise men find the child,
With gold, myrrh, frankincense they come
To Him, the undefiled.

4. Your God is here, in honest toil,
A carpenter by trade,
No imperfection there to spoil
His deity displayed.

5. Your God is Love, beside the sea
In city and in mart,
To teach and heal and set men free,
And soothe the broken heart.

6. Your God is here, upon the tree,
Unwanted, bruised and torn,
The Scripture says it was for thee
this cruelty was borne.

7. Your God is here, in garden tomb,
To bear your sin He died,
But now He breaks from that dark womb,
Raised up and glorified.

8. Your God is here this Christmas morn,
Don't lose Him in the throng,
It was for you that He was born,
Come praise him in this song:

9. All glory be to God on high
And praise to Christ the Son,
The Holy Spirit brings us nigh,
Praise God, the Three in One.

10. At His first Advent we rejoice,
Then look with eager eye,
Proclaiming Him with heart and voice
Whose coming draweth nigh.

11. The second Advent soon will come,
May we for Him prepare,
For he will take His people home;
His glory we will share.

Music © 2013 Harry Hicks
Words © 2013 Brenda Gallant

46 Your life is borrowed

Brenda Gallant　　　　　　　　　　　　　　　　　　　　Harry Hicks

Your life is bor-rowed from the Lord, He made you for His own,
So why not heed His Ho-ly Word, And make your Heart His throne?

2. The human heart is dead in sin
'Till quickened from above,
Then His new life will reign within;
The outcome of His love.

3. Until that time the soul is lost,
And wandering on alone,
But, oh, at what an awesome cost,
The soul is sought and won.

4. He came right down to where we are,
Leaving His throne on high,
And even though we wandered far,
He sought to bring us nigh.

5. Will you respond to His dear voice?
Now is the time choose.
If you make the Lord your choice,
Your life he'll surely use.

6. It won't be long 'till His return
To snatch His own away,
Do not His invitation spurn,
Be ready for that day!

Music © 2013 Harry Hicks
Words © 2013 Brenda Gallant

Made in the USA
Charleston, SC
31 August 2014